# ROCKS AND MINERALS

KINGFISHER
NEW YORK

Consultant: Douglas Palmer

Designed and created by Basher www.basherworld.com

Dedicated to Jos Marbrook


Published in the United States by Kingfisher
175 Fifth Avenue, New York, NY 10010
Kingfisher is an imprint of Macmillan Children's Books, London.


Distributed in the U.S. by Macmillan, 175 Fifth Ave., New York, NY 10010
Distributed in Canada by H.B. Fenn and Company Ltd., 34 Nixon Road,
Bolton, Ontario L7E 1W2

Library of Congress Cataloging-in-Publication Data has been applied for.

ISBN: 978-0-7534-6314-7

Kingfisher books are available for special promotions and premiums.
For details contact: Special Markets Department, Macmillan,
175 Fifth Avenue, New York, NY 10010.

For more information, please visit www.kingfisherpublications.com

First American Edition September 2009
Printed in Taiwan
9 8 7 6 5 4 3 2 1
1TR/0609/SHENS/SC/126.6MA/C

# CONTENTS

# Introduction

## Geology/Charles Lyell

Geology is the most down-to-earth of all the sciences. It's gritty and lets you get your hands dirty. You may not have realized it, but the rocks and minerals under our feet hold the secrets of our planet. Understanding where they come from and how they form helps us answer questions about how Earth fits in with the solar system, how long it has been here, and how we came to live on it.

Finding out Earth's age was the most important piece of this puzzle, and the quiet man behind the scenes was Charles Lyell (1797–1875). The grandfather of geology championed the idea that processes happening on Earth today must also have operated in the same way, and at the same rate, in the past. The steady trickle of water—from the sky, glaciers, rivers, and seas—can level mountain ranges. New bedrock can be laid down grain by grain, and slow changes in sea levels can swamp entire continents or make new landmasses rise from the sea. Since Lyell's time, we have learned a lot, including the effects of meteor impacts and about Earth's moving plates. Geology is a subject that can really rock your world!

Charles Lyell

# CHAPTER 1

## Sedimentary and Stylish

Handsome in their honeyed tones, this group of dapper dressers drape themselves over 80 percent of Earth's land area. Most of them are clastic (made from pieces of other rocks). When rocks are worn away by wind and rain, the broken-off pieces get transported down toward the seas by glaciers and rivers. They're dumped when rivers lack the energy to carry them any farther. Particles and fragments build up like a layer cake as more debris piles on top. The long burial process squeezes the water out of this massive spongy sediment, turning it into solid rock.

Clay

Shale

Limestone

Flint

Sandstone

Conglomerate

Evaporite

Coal

# Clay

## Sedimentary and Stylish

- A clastic rock formed from tiny particles of clay minerals
- This sloppy and gloppy character is used in facial masks
- Forms a barrier to liquids, so it's good for blocking dams

I am a real smoothie. A delicate mix of the finest grains, I'm the type of mushy goo that can suck rain boots off your feet. My main ingredients are tiny particles that you can't see unless you use an electron microscope. Because my particles are so light, I go with the flow. I get carried far and wide by streams, rivers, and seas, only coming to rest in the most tranquil, low-energy environments. I coat the bottoms of lakes and lagoons. I build up very slowly, blanketing huge areas.

When I dry out, I crack and become rock hard—and this is my most useful trait. Thousands of years ago, humans learned to craft objects from wet clay and then fire them in kilns to make them durable. With bricks, tiles, cement, and all kinds of pottery, I really sent them to pieces!

- Minerals: kaolinite, smectite, illite
- Grain size: very fine
- Hardness: 2–3
- Color: gray, blue, red, brown, yellow
- Texture: stretchy when wet
- Look-alike: mudstone

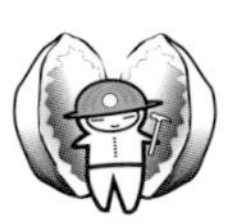

Clay

# Shale

## Sedimentary and Stylish

- A splintery rock made from weathering of other clastic rocks
- An everywhere man, it's Earth's most common sedimentary rock
- Containing so many fossils, it's a one-stop shop for fossil hunters

My experiences in becoming a rock have been brutal. I'm made from the same particles as Clay, but I've been under pressure, which has compressed and hardened me. Any more pressure and I'd turn into Slate! I was laid down at the bottom of deep oceans, shallow seas, and floodplains. The bodies of dead animals sank to the depths along with a rain of fine particles, making me a favorite rock for fossil hunters. Bones, shells, leafy imprints, and the track marks of ancient beasts, such as trilobites, are common in the flat layers of my bedding planes.

Like Clay, I am used for roof tiles, bricks, and pottery, but I need to be ground up first. Sometimes I am found in greasy slabs called oil shale. If you could find a cheap way to squeeze the oil from my layers, I'd make you rich.

- Minerals: kaolinite, smectite, illite
- Grain size: very fine
- Hardness: 3
- Color: gray, brown, green, red
- Common name: clay-rich mudstone
- Look-alike: Slate

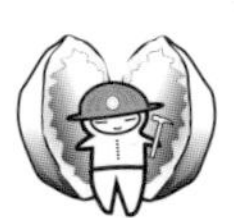

Shale

# Limestone

## Sedimentary and Stylish

- A milky white, calcium-containing sedimentary rock
- This old rock provided homes for ancient cavemen
- An organic, tropical soul, often made from dead sea creatures

Graceful in sheer white, I form in balmy shallow seas, where calcium carbonate is laid down as soft mud. I am made up of pieces of coral reefs and seashells (shelly limestone), the tiny shells of free-floating creatures (chalk), or delicately rolled spheres of calcite (oolitic limestone). When I become solid rock, I take shape as giant blocks many feet high, dominating hillsides and forming cliffs.

I'm long-lived, and I make a good building material, but I dissolve easily in acid. Even rain can carve through me, which is why limestone areas are riddled with caves and potholes. When dissolved in water, I make your water hard and crust up your showerhead. I am an essential ingredient in cement, and I'm burned to produce quicklime, which is used in fertilizers and glassmaking.

- Mineral: calcite
- Grain size: fine to coarse
- Hardness: 4
- Color: white, gray, yellow, red
- Texture: bedded with fossils
- Look-alike: none

Limestone

# Flint

## Sedimentary and Stylish

- The glassy firebrand queen of the Stone Age
- Found in strange nodules and concretions
- Made of silica and develops in limestone as it hardens

My friends call me Flinty. A hard and pitiless rock, I deserve my name. I dress in dark colors of black, gray, and deep brown to show that I'm not to be messed with, and when struck, I make sparks fly. Made entirely of silica—the stuff of sand and quartz—and with no internal structure, I can be "knapped" (honed to a sharp edge). Stone Age people made their axes, knives, and arrowheads from me. Later on, gun makers exploited my explosive talents in flintlock muskets, where I provided the spark to ignite gunpowder.

A strange and complicated character, I'm always found mixed in with big softies such as Limestone. I come in weird blobby nodules. Houses and walls made from chunks of me are virtually indestructible.

- Mineral: quartz
- Grain size: very fine
- Hardness: 6.5
- Color: black, brown, gray, green
- Origin: oceans and seas
- Look-alike: Obsidian

Flint

# Sandstone

## Sedimentary and Stylish

- A clastic rock, formed from sandy pieces of other rocks
- Its aquifers hold life-giving water beneath Earth's surface
- It's Earth's second-most-common sedimentary rock

Surf's up! Made of the sand that gets into your picnic food, I'm a rock dressed in warm golds and tans. I am one of nature's finest features, running the length of the Grand Canyon. A rock with true grit, I am made up of particles of quartz with a cement of silica or calcium carbonate in between my grains. I get laid down where sand collects, on riverbeds and beaches. The ripples within my bedding planes are clues to my origin. Long, angular ripples form in windblown sand dunes, and tidal deposits give shorter, more even waves.

Warm colored and easy to shape, I am a top-grade stone for building and paving. I'm also a dab hand at sharpening steel blades. On top of that, I can store a huge amount of water in the spaces between my grains.

- Minerals: quartz, feldspar
- Grain size: very fine to coarse
- Hardness: 6.5–7
- Color: white, gray, yellow, red, brown
- Origin: deserts, rivers, seas
- Look-alikes: siltstone, oolite

Sandstone

# Conglomerate

## Sedimentary and Stylish

- A coarse-grained clastic rock and a complete fruitcake
- A chip off the old block found in high-energy environments
- *Conglomerate* means "a gathering of different things"

I have pudding for brains. I'm a jumbled mix of lumpy pieces encased in a stew of finer particles. Unlike my brother, breccia, I am a well-rounded fellow. You can tell us apart because I contain smoothed-off stones, while his lumpy parts are spiky and angular.

I am made out of leftover rocks—those that have been broken and carried away by rivers, waves, earthquakes, glaciers, and landslides. Sometimes I hold only a single rock type, but more often I'm a mix of different rocks and minerals. To find out about me, check my lumps and bumps. Most obvious is the type of stone (source rock) that broke up to make me. The size of my pebbles can tell you how well traveled I am. Well-sorted, rounded pebbles will have trekked farther from the original source.

- Minerals: mixed
- Grain size: coarse
- Hardness: variable
- Color: bright yellow, red, gray
- Common name: puddingstone
- Look-alike: breccia

Conglomerate

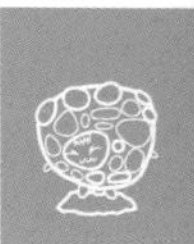

# Evaporite

## ■ Sedimentary and Stylish

- This chemical sediment isn't like other sedimentary rocks
- Rock salt is the most famous evaporite, along with rock gypsum
- Salt mines were used to hide works of art during World War II

I am a special salty sea dog! No other rock forms like me. In dry regions, where only limited fresh water flows into lakes or shallow seas, I begin to dry out. As the water evaporates, the minerals dissolved in it become concentrated, making the lake salty. The minerals crystallize and fall to the lakebed, like the dregs at the bottom of a teacup. Eventually, the layers of minerals left behind become rock. I form immense beds in between layers of more solid rock. Because I'm just a little more flexible, I can trap large underground reservoirs of oil and natural gas under vast domes of salt.

Most rock salt ends up in your food—I'm essential for life. I'm also important to the chemical industry for hydrochloric acid, plastics, and plaster of Paris.

- Minerals: gypsum, halite
- Grain size: fine to coarse
- Hardness: 2–2.5
- Color: bright red, yellow, white
- Deposits: Great Salt Lake, Utah
- Look-alike: none

Evaporite

# Coal

## Sedimentary and Stylish

- A fiery fellow, mined from underground seams and open pits
- This organic rock forms from long-dead plant matter
- A smoky fossil fuel that is killing our planet when burned

I am a grubby, smudgy character with a warm heart. I'm formed when dead plant material in swampy forests is stopped from rotting away. As it is buried, it is squeezed and forms peat—a soft dark brown soil. With increasing pressure, I become blacker, harder, and better for burning. My densest type is called anthracite. A large amount of Earth's coal was formed in the swampy Carboniferous period (354–290 million years ago).

I am the most important rock in the world! Generating much of your electricity, I'm the only rock that can keep you toasty during the winter! I also belch out lots of carbon dioxide. Because you humans rely on me for energy, the scarcer I become, the more costly I get. You'd better behave or you'll get a lump of me for Christmas!

- Mineral: carbon
- Grain size: very fine
- Hardness: 2
- Color: black, brown
- Largest coal mine: Black Thunder, Wyo.
- Look-alikes: Obsidian, chert

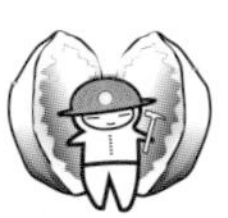

Coal

# CHAPTER 2

## Molten Maniacs

This hot group start out as liquid rock deep within Earth. If they reach the surface, these firebrands run amuck—they spill out over the ground as lava and explode out of volcanoes. Columns of dusty ash and molten rock race down mountains, causing death and destruction. When their tempers cool, these guys form a solid matrix of interlocking crystals. They make up 95 percent of Earth's crust—on land they often have a thin covering of other rocks, but they dominate the ocean floor. Many of the world's most important minerals are found in them.

Granite

Diorite

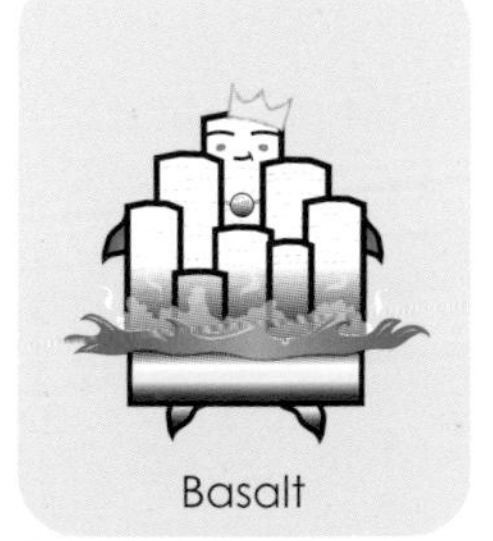
Basalt

Peridotite

Obsidian

Tuff

Pumice

Meteorite

# Granite

## Molten Maniacs

- Heavy-duty rock that underpins Earth's continental crust
- A coarse-grained rock found everywhere
- An intrusive rock, which means that it solidifies underground

Chunky and built to last, I'm the stuff that mountains are made of. I form the backbone of Earth's continents, a solid hunk on which the thin skin of sedimentary rocks sits. I crystallize, turning from liquid into solid rock, dozens of miles under the surface. I appear in huge bubbles of cooling magma called batholiths, which can be hundreds of miles across. I am so tough that as other rock layers around me are stripped away by wind, rain, and weather, I stand tall as impressive mountain ranges.

My interlocking light and dark crystals give me a speckled look. I come in pink, reds, and blacks, and I can be polished. I am the most hard-wearing natural building material. You see me adorning the façades of many important buildings and on kitchen counters.

- Minerals: feldspar, quartz, mica
- Grain size: coarse
- Hardness: 6
- Color: black, gray, pink, red, yellow
- Granite State: New Hampshire
- Look-alikes: Diorite, Gneiss

Granite

# Diorite

## Molten Maniacs

- Dark and mottled tough guy with coarse grains
- Related to Granite and sometimes called black granite
- Intrusive, like Granite, but not as widespread

On first impression, you could be forgiven for thinking that I was an upmarket Granite, but I'm a different sort of rock. I'm darker and sleeker. My grains are smaller and more beautiful. I'm still a salt-and-pepper rock, but I contain little quartz. I'm mainly made of light feldspar and dark hornblende. I form underground, but if I reach the surface, I erupt as a thick, lumpy lava that is dangerously explosive. When the lava cools, it's called andesite, after the Andes Mountains in South America.

I'm a tougher customer than Granite and a polished performer, too. The ancient Egyptians loved me. I was prized because my dark surface can hold a shine very well. My hardness means that I don't scratch easily, and inscriptions carved into me last for thousands of years.

- Minerals: plagioclase, hornblende
- Grain size: coarse
- Hardness: 7
- Color: dark gray, green
- Where used: Egyptian statues
- Look-alikes: diabase, gabbro

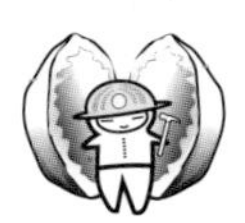

Diorite

# Basalt

## Molten Maniacs

- This king of the seas is a high-spirited extrusive lava
- The most common volcanic rock, and a part-time island maker
- The Moon's dark patches are made of basalt

Don't be put off by my dull gray appearance—I'm an extrovert at heart who makes islands for fun. In November 1963, I made the brand-new island of Surtsey, near Iceland, in just a few days. I'm found under the oceans all over the world. My individual crystals are almost too small to see because I am made from lava that cooled too quickly for them to grow. With a great release of pressure, I bubble to the surface with bits of peridotite.

I create some of the world's wackiest rock shapes. My runny lava forms coiled rock ropes called pahoehoe (say "pah-hoy-hoy") and hollow lava tubes. I make pillowy lumps when I spill out from underwater volcanoes. I also made the Giant's Causeway in Ireland—its pipe-organ-shaped columns formed as I cooled.

- Minerals: plagioclase, augite
- Grain size: fine
- Hardness: 6–7
- Color: black, dark gray
- Surtsey's size: 0.5 sq. mi. (1.4 km$^2$)
- Look-alikes: glassy volcanic rocks

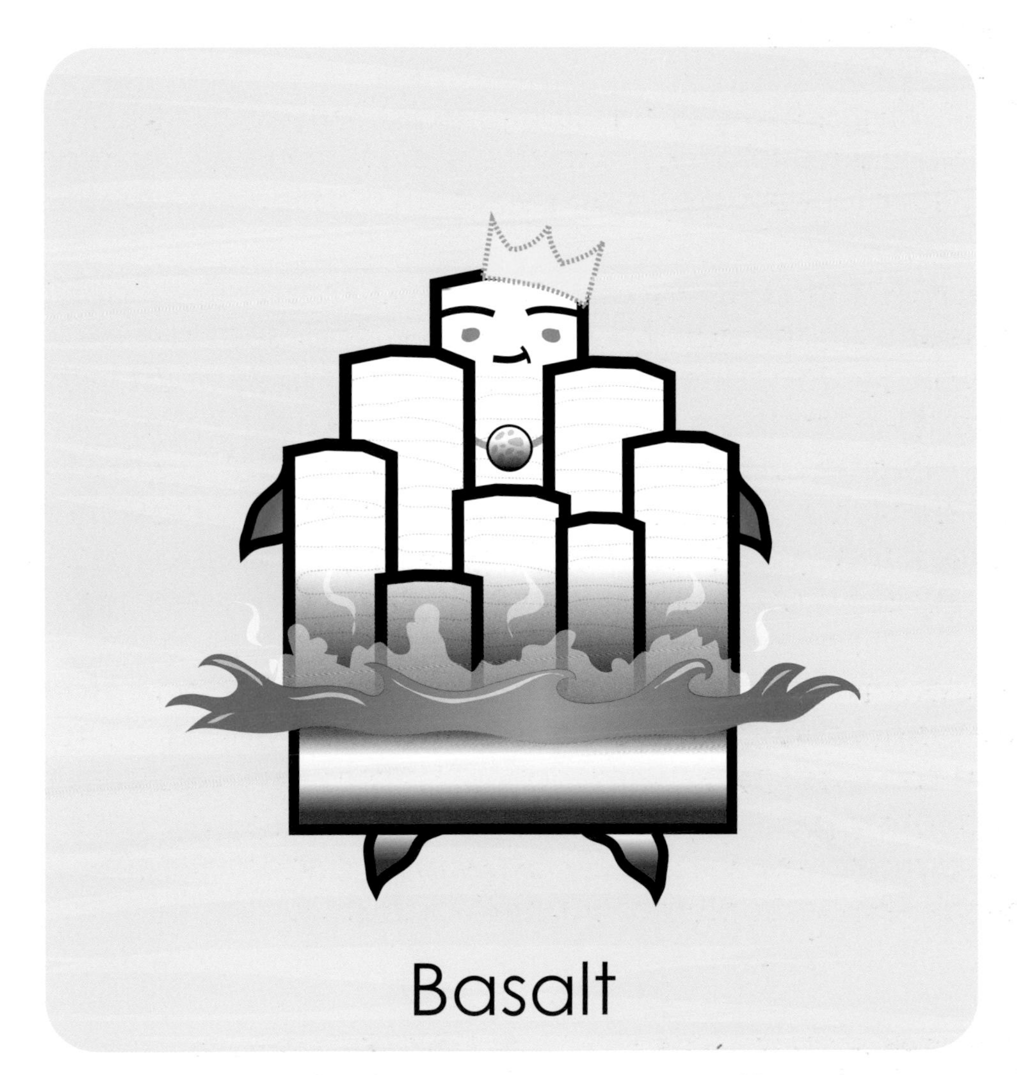

Basalt

# Peridotite

## Molten Maniacs

- Green giant who comes from deep down
- This intrusive fellow is the main player in Earth's molten mantle
- Earth's tectonic plates slide slowly on this hidden operator

I have hidden depths. Like an iceberg, there is a lot going on beneath the surface. I am the big cheese down to 250 mi. (400km) deep. Even the tectonic plates that scoot around on Earth's surface have about 60 mi. (100km) worth of me on their undersides. But I'm a rare bird on the surface—mostly seen in stacked, layered sandwiches of rock that are scraped off oceanic plates as they disappear back to the depths at subduction zones.

I bring gemstones and precious metals up to the surface with me. I contain Earth's largest deposits of chromium and am associated with platinum, the world's most expensive metal. I'm found in South Africa's kimberlite pipes, mixed in with lovely diamonds, and I have my own gemstone—a glassy green beauty called peridot.

- Minerals: olivine, pyroxene
- Grain size: fine to coarse
- Hardness: 6.5–7
- Color: green, gray
- Source of: peridot
- Look-alike: Eclogite

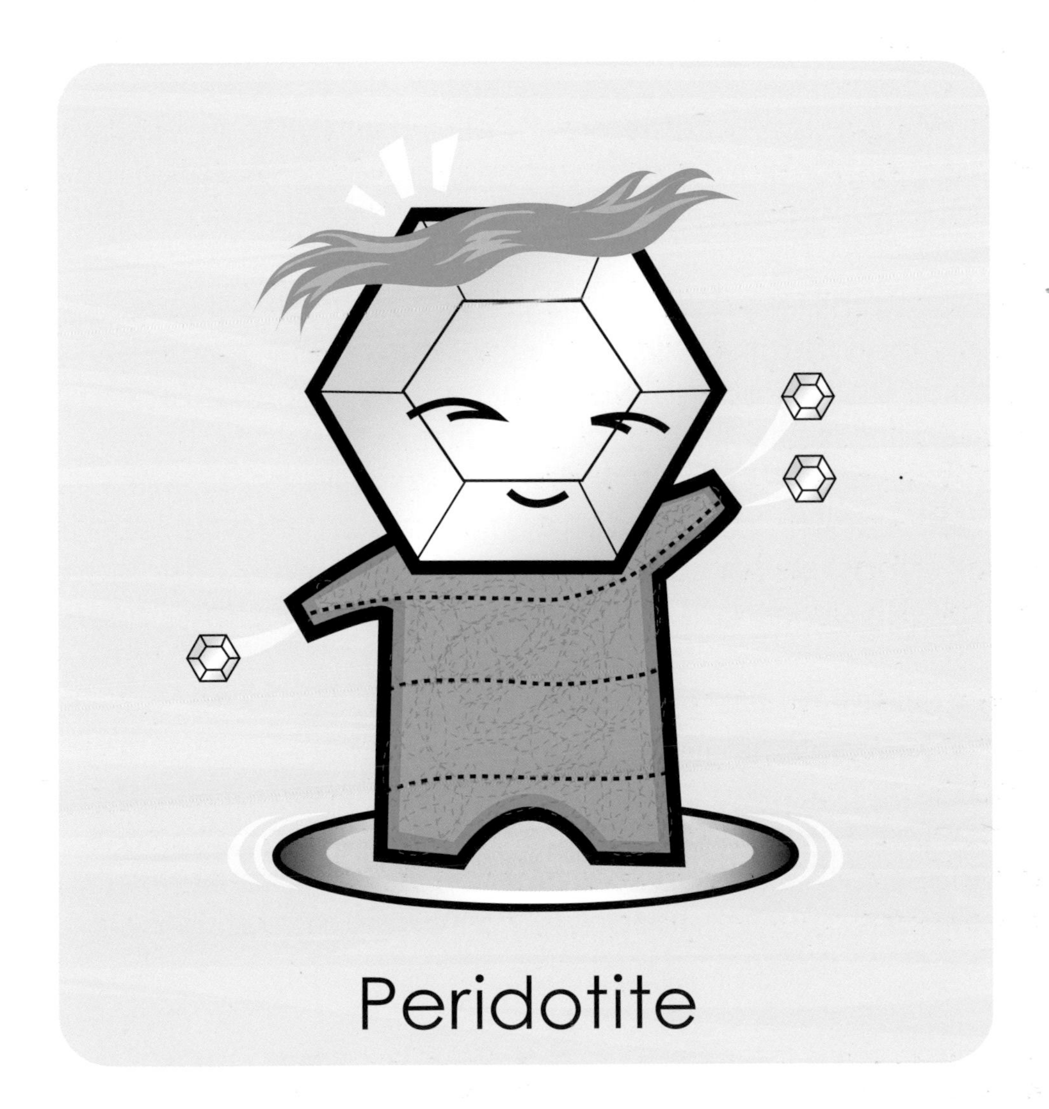

Peridotite

# Obsidian

## Molten Maniacs

- Stunning volcanic glass important to the Native Americans
- Sharper than steel, this is a real cutting-edge material
- Since it degrades with time, it's never over 20 million years old

Black as night and dangerous to know, I'm a sharp, pointy individual. My frosted-glass surface gives away nothing about my makeup. I have the same chemical composition as Granite, but I'm not a true rock. I am a firm-set liquid—a little like jelly but squillions of times harder. As I rise from underground toward the surface, I lose almost all the water I contain, becoming thick and gloppy. Even an ant could outrun one of my lava flows.

You can tell by the way I fracture that I have no internal crystal arrangement. I break with jagged edges, so I can be chipped, whittled, and honed to give me a cruel cutting edge. This skill has been used for thousands of years to make ceremonial and sacrificial knives and today for surgical blades.

- Minerals: quartz, feldspar
- Grain size: fine
- Hardness: 5.5
- Color: dark colors, white features
- Where found: young lava flows
- Look-alikes: Flint, chert

Obsidian

# Tuff

## Molten Maniacs

- A mixed-up mess burped out of a volcano
- This pasty pale, ashen character is found on crater walls
- It mixes with vile volcanic gases to sickening effect

Tuff by name, I'm the meanest Maniac. When volcanoes erupt, they spit out all kinds of stuff, from ash to molten rock. I am made mostly of ash. Each particle is light, but as a mass they hit like a freight train, and at more than 1,450°F (800°C), the flow vaporizes everything in its path—like when Mount Vesuvius erupted in Italy in A.D. 79, encasing the people of Pompeii in tough shells of ash.

- Minerals: silica, rock fragments
- Grain size: fine to coarse
- Hardness: variable
- Color: brown, gray, yellow, red
- Where found: young volcanoes
- Look-alike: ignimbrite

# Pumice

## Molten Maniacs

- Bubbly character thrown out when volcanoes blow their tops
- This cotton-candy airhead can float in water for a year or more
- It forms huge floating rafts, providing homes for sea creatures

I'm a light, frothy fellow who's proud to be the only rock that floats. Full of holes, I am 90 percent cavities with smooth walls. Being the result of volcanic explosions, I'm often found with my buddy Obsidian but can also be found far away from volcanoes because I drift with the tide. I'm a great scrubber, with many uses—polishing, erasing, and taking dead skin off your feet!

- Mineral: silica
- Grain size: fine
- Hardness: 6, but friable
- Color: light gray, cream, white
- Where found: young volcanoes
- Look-alike: diatomite

# Meteorite

## Molten Maniacs

- Cold, remote fellow who comes from asteroids or Mars rocks
- Each meteorite is named after the location in which it is found
- The big busters, called bolides, cause global devastation

I'm a screaming banshee, fast, wild, and free. I ride the winds of the solar system until I hit Earth and come howling through the atmosphere like a bolt from the blue. The crucial difference between me and your average shooting star is that I'm a survivor. Traveling through the atmosphere at such a speed burns up smaller shooting stars, but I live to tell the tale.

Some scientists say I brought life to Earth, but more often I bring death and destruction. A massive meteorite crashed down millions of years ago and probably sent the dinosaurs into extinction. Talk about coming down to Earth with a bang! After eons of spinning through the icy wastes of space, I offer scientists clues about the materials that formed the planets in the solar system.

- Minerals: pyroxene, olivine
- Grain size: fine to coarse
- Hardness: 7
- Color: dark gray, blue, green
- Largest: Hoba, Namibia (66 tons)
- Look-alikes: gabbro, Peridotite

Meteorite

# CHAPTER 3

## The Metamorphics

Now you see 'em, now you don't—this bunch of mighty morphing shape shifters start out as one type of rock but change when heated up or put under pressure. This happens with contact metamorphism—when the Molten Maniacs are nearby—or regional metamorphism, during periods of mountain building when Earth's massive plates grind into one another. Metamorphics can change so much that they become unrecognizable from their original rocks. Because Earth's rock chemistry is a mixed bag, there is an almost infinite range of results.

Quartzite

Slate

Marble

Schist

Gneiss

Eclogite

# Quartzite

## The Metamorphics

- A gray-white or pinkish rock made from sandstone
- So hard wearing that it's at the surface for billions of years
- Often formed when Earth's tectonic plates grind together

Nothing wears me down—I'm the definition of true grit! Like any superhero, I started out life as an ordinary character. I was a sandstone, but everything changed when I was buried deep within Earth, squeezed and baked at high temperatures.

Invincibility is woven into my very fabric. In the pressure cooker underneath the plates, my individual sandy grains, and the cement binding them together, recrystallized into an interlocking fortress of quartz crystal. A lot like hardened oatmeal on the side of a bowl, I'm immovable, which is why some of the oldest rocks on Earth are made of me. The quartzites in Western Australia are a mind-boggling 3.5 billion years old! I also make an excellent base on which to build railroad tracks.

- Mineral: quartz
- Grain size: fine to coarse
- Hardness: 7
- Color: white, gray, brown, reddish
- Pressure: low; temperature: high
- Look-alike: Sandstone

Quartzite

# Slate

## The Metamorphics

- Low-grade metamorphic rock, like Shale but much harder
- A smooth operator quarried worldwide for its evenness
- Comes in many surprising colors, such as green and purple

You might think of me as dull—slate gray—and all that. I have humble origins, true, but like a butterfly, I have metamorphosed into something beautiful. I was once an everyday sedimentary rock—a clay, a mudstone, or a volcanic ash. But given a little pressure, something remarkable happened—my minerals shifted and began to realign themselves in the direction of the force.

Because my flattened minerals stack up on top of one another, I have two sets of layers: my first sedimentary set, called bedding, and a new metamorphic set, called foliation. I split easily in this direction, producing crisp, flat surfaces. This makes me a versatile material. I've always been used for roofing. I also make the best playing surfaces for pool tables.

- Minerals: quartz, mica, feldspar
- Grain size: very fine
- Hardness: 2.5–5.5
- Color: dark gray, green, purple
- Pressure: low; temperature: low
- Look-alike: none

Slate

# Marble

## The Metamorphics

- A sugary pretty boy formed by metamorphism of limestone
- Hard, smooth, and with wedding-cake tones; can be valuable
- Name comes from the Greek word meaning "shining stone"

Although it's not in my nature to boast, I've got the looks. Waxy and clear, my flawless complexion drives artists and architects wild. I was a favorite for triumphal buildings during the Roman Empire. I've even caused international incidents, such as when the Elgin Marbles were removed from the Acropolis in Athens, Greece, and taken to England.

Because I'm made from sedimentary limestone, I come in huge blocks without any foliation (metamorphic layering), which is why I'm great to carve. I'm often formed as I'm cooked by heat and pressure, and my grains of calcite become interlocking crystals of calcite. This is called contact metamorphism. These changes can also happen with deep burial. You can find me in kitchen counters, fireplaces, and tiles.

- Mineral: calcite
- Grain size: coarse
- Hardness: 4–5
- Color: a large variety
- Pressure: moderate; temperature: high
- Look-alike: Limestone

Marble

# Schist

## The Metamorphics

- A groovy dude known for its flakiness and inner flaws
- Made of the same stuff as Clay, Shale, and Slate, but harder
- Its colors indicate pressure and heat when it formed

I wrap myself in a glinting coat that shimmers in the sun. I'm made of average minerals, such as mica, but it can look like I am bursting with flakes of diamond or ruby-red garnet crystals. I come from all types of rocks, from clays to granites, but I have been under horrific pressure and heat. My new minerals shave off easily, but I'm still used as a building material.

- Minerals: quartz, feldspar, mica
- Grain size: fine
- Hardness: 4–5
- Color: light gray, green, red
- Pressure: high; temperature: high
- Look-alike: banded Gneiss

# Gneiss

## The Metamorphics

- A coarse-grained, high-grade rock, often mistaken for Granite
- This "gneiss" guy looks like a layer cake—a total grain-iac!
- A hardy mountain rock found in the world's major ranges

Unlike that showoff Schist, I go to extremes. Trapped in between two tectonic plates in the earth, I am forged by crushing forces. The huge pressure remodels my minerals, pressing them into distinct dark and pale bands. The bands are then squished into a jellyroll look. Long lasting, I am often used to replace granite as an inexpensive building stone.

- Minerals: feldspar, quartz
- Grain size: coarse
- Hardness: 6
- Color: bands of gray and pink
- Pressure: high; temperature: high
- Look-alikes: Granite, Schist

# Eclogite

## The Metamorphics

- A very rare character who is often unstable at the surface
- Made from basalt dragged into Earth's hot mantle
- An extremist who provides a force for mantle convection

I can take the pain and strain. I never crack under pressure. I am the highest grade of Metamorphics! Made from pink-red garnet crystals surrounded by greenish clinopyroxene, I'm one of the rarest rocks.

It's impossible to create me in Earth's crust—the pressures at which I form are found only in the mantle. I'm made at subduction zones, where tectonic plates spear down into the mantle. As the forces build on Earth's crust, it heats up, turning into me and becoming 10 percent more dense. This drags the crust deeper into Earth, so it's a mystery how I appear at the surface at all! One idea is that the force of the descending cold plate drives the circulation of hot liquid rocks within the mantle, which brings up a chunk or two of my alien material.

- Minerals: garnet, clinopyroxene
- Grain size: medium to coarse
- Hardness: 5–6
- Color: red, gray, green
- Pressure: high; temperature: high
- Look-alike: none

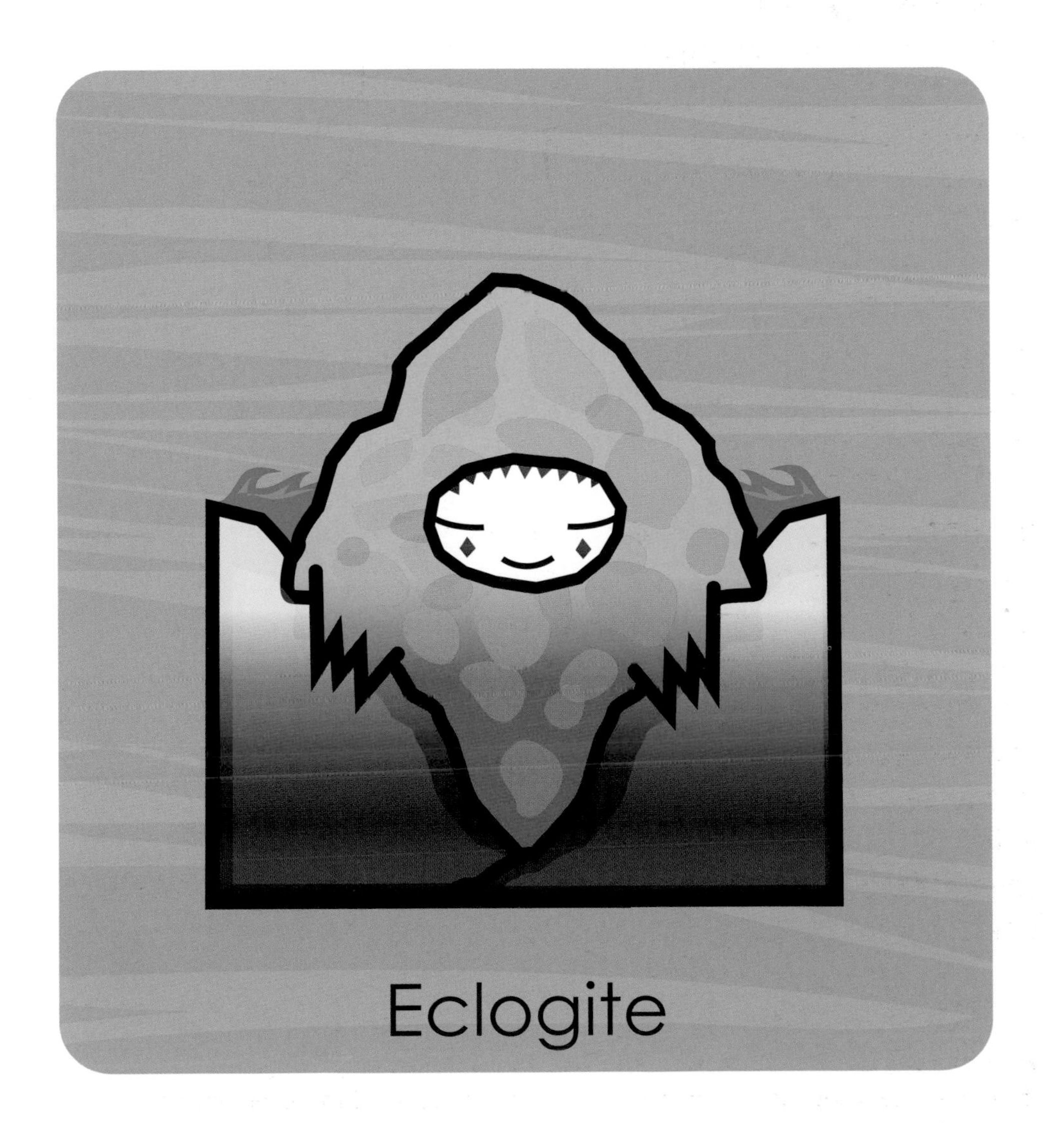
Eclogite

# CHAPTER 4
## Shock and Ore

Totally "ore-some," these are the moneymakers of the mineral world. These wealthy weasels include most of Earth's metals. From steel (iron) for construction to copper for conducting electricity, this bunch have helped build the modern world. Their valuable material is locked inside their crystal matrix and mixed up with worthless rocks, but processing them yields the prize. These impure deposits are even more expensive than the elemental Purists because they are extremely scarce. Billions of dollars are spent every year tracking down new reserves.

Pyrite

Hematite

Magnetite

Uraninite

Galena

Chalcopyrite

# Pyrite

## Shock and Ore

- This guy grows in cubes, but he's no square
- Makes beautiful fossils by "pyritization" of dead animal cells
- Rusty patches on rocks are often caused by me

I'm a self-styled comedian! I love a good prank, and my best one is that I look a lot like Gold. But I'm one of the most common minerals, so the joke's on you if you think you've struck it rich—my other name is Fool's Gold!

I might not be a golden boy, but I am the most common sulfide mineral in Earth's crust. I don't often give away my secrets, but since you've been so kind as to read about me, here's how to tell me apart from Gold. In large lumps of me, it's easy to see I grow in cubes. I'm much harder than that sissy Gold—only good-quality steel will scratch me. I can also be found out by the fishy smell I give off when I'm pounded into powder. I'm often with my best buddy, Chalcopyrite. I also hang out with Coal and sometimes even with the real stuff, too!

- Made of: iron sulfide
- Chemical formula: $FeS_2$
- Hardness: 6–6.5
- Color: brassy gold
- Crystal system: cubic
- Look-alikes: Chalcopyrite, Gold

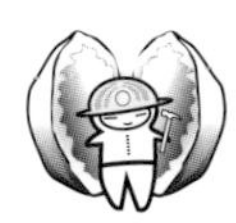

Pyrite

# Hematite

## Shock and Ore

- Red of tooth and claw, this mineral doesn't mix in with rocks
- Magnetite reacts with oxygen in the air to produce this guy
- The name *Hematite* comes from the Greek word meaning "blood"

Like the blood in your veins, I'm a rich source of iron. Used to make steel, iron is the world's most important metal, and with a 70 percent iron content, an ore like me is second to none. I have a range of costumes, which makes me tricky to spot. I can come dressed in metallic gray with a soft sheen or as gleaming six-sided crystals (called rhomboids). My most recognizable form is smooth, rounded kidneys—I kidney you not! The best way to test for me is to crush me. My powder is blood red and forms the base of the red pigment ocher.

I'm used to polish gemstones and am found in some of the oldest rocks on Earth, the banded iron formation (BIF). The BIFs are everywhere, from North and South America to Asia and Australia. I was even found on Mars.

- Made of: iron oxide
- Chemical formula: $Fe_2O_3$
- Hardness: 5–6
- Color: steel gray
- Crystal system: hexagonal, trigonal
- Look-alike: pyrolusite

Hematite

# Magnetite

## Shock and Ore

- A shady character found on black-sand beaches
- This mineral had a star turn in the theory of plate tectonics
- Migrating birds and dolphins use this guy to help find their way

With my superhero name, I'm a man of steel with a magnetic personality. POW! An important iron ore, I'm found in vast quantities all over the world in igneous, metamorphic, and sedimentary banded iron formations. I'm the most magnetic of all natural minerals. I can be used for magnetic compasses, but my maverick ways can also send compasses haywire.

- Made of: iron oxide
- Chemical formula: $Fe_3O_4$
- Hardness: 5.5
- Color: black, brown
- Crystal system: cubic
- Look-alike: chromite

# Uraninite

## Shock and Ore

- A powerhouse of hidden and dangerous potential
- The Curies found a new element, radium, in this fellow
- Most nuclear power plants use uranium recycled from bombs

I am a radioactive renegade. Dark and pulsating, I'm the principal ore of uranium, which fuels nuclear power. No one guessed my value until 1898, when radium was discovered. I am often found with Silver, and German silver miners called me "pitchblende" because of my dark looks and because they thought nothing useful could be extracted from me.

- Made of: uranium oxide
- Chemical formula: $UO_2$
- Hardness: 4–6
- Color: black, brown
- Crystal system: cubic
- Look-alike: none

# Galena

## Shock and Ore

- This toxic terror has a long and distinguished history
- Galena was used in the first crystal radio sets
- Lead is extracted from the rock ore by smelting

Get a "lode" of me! I'm the chief ore of the heavy metal lead, and there's no mistaking me—I'm eight sides of mean-looking crystals with an oily blue-black sheen. Mostly found in lodes or veins along with Silver, I go back a long way. One of my first uses was as kohl in ancient Egypt—a kind of (poisonous) eye shadow used to ward off flies and the sun's glare. Because lead is soft and easy to work with, the Romans extracted the metal from me to use in pipes and paints—it leached out into the water supply and could build up to lethal levels in the body.

These days, lead is still used for roofing, but you're more likely to find it in batteries and as shields against x-rays. I am also a semiconductor of electricity, which means that I'm a sparky addition to electronic transistors.

- Made of: lead sulfide
- Chemical formula: PbS
- Hardness: 2.5
- Color: dark silvery gray
- Crystal system: cubic
- Look-alike: argentite

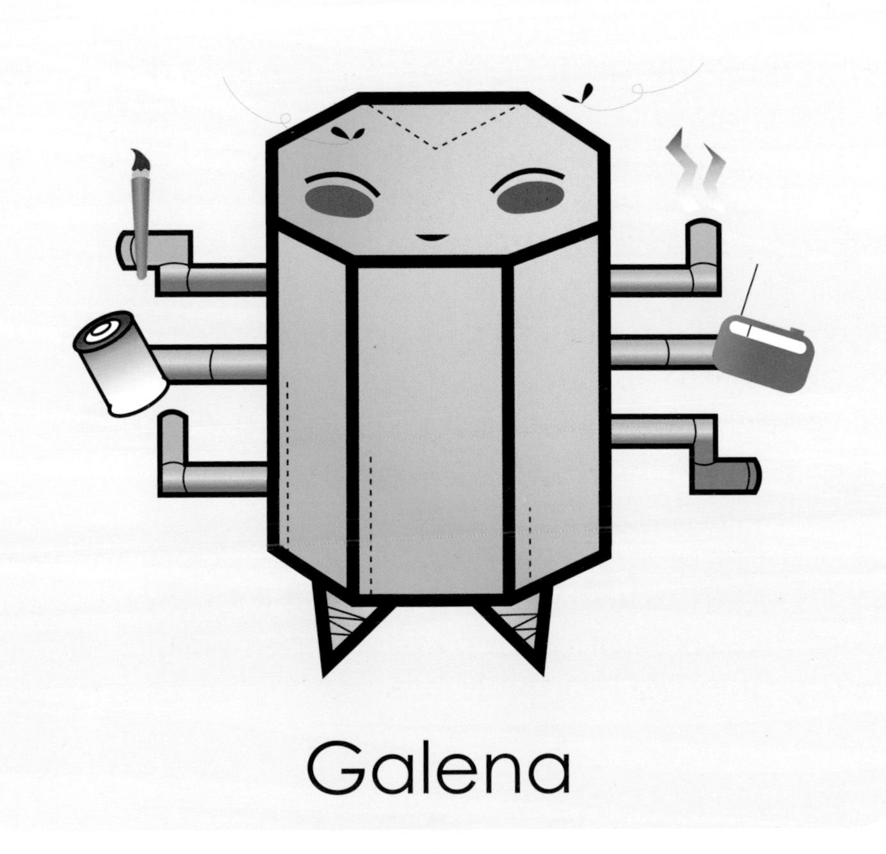
Galena

# Chalcopyrite

## Shock and Ore

- Eighty percent of the world's copper is held in this ore mineral
- Found in many igneous rocks but also in coal seams
- This copper-bottomed character is often mixed up with Pyrite

I am the most important ore of copper and, I'd like to think, the most important mineral ore of all. First up, you should know how to say my name—it's "kal-co-pie-right." I'm sometimes called "yellow copper," but I'm more brassy gold, so I'm often confused with Pyrite. It doesn't help that I'm thick as thieves with that maverick, and we are often found together in the same deposits. You can see me in copper blooms—bright green snotty trails all over a rock surface, like ectoplasmic splatter from an alien.

It's almost impossible to list all the uses of copper when it's been extracted, but without me, there'd be no electrical wires and your water pipes would still be made of lethal lead!

- Made of: copper iron sulfide
- Chemical formula: $CuFeS_2$
- Hardness: 2.5–3
- Color: brassy
- Crystal system: tetragonal
- Look-alikes: bornite, Gold, Pyrite

Chalcopyrite

# CHAPTER 5
## Mineral Gang

Welcome to this fascinating group of earthy treasures! There are more than 3,000 of these fellows—each one with a unique structure and chemical composition. A mineral's chemistry is mostly so orderly that its atoms fit together in a repeated 3-D pattern that forms crystals. These guys occur in veins hundreds of feet—even miles—long. The Mineral Gang often share similar structures, and they can morph from one into another. Fluid flowing through rocks can bring new atoms into the mix, altering a crystal's chemical makeup.

Quartz

Opal

Agate

Feldspar

Olivine

Tourmaline

Augite

Hornblende

Mica

Serpentine

Talc

Kaolinite

Garnet

Gypsum

Calcite

Malachite

Apatite

Fluorite

# Quartz

## Mineral Gang

- An itchy, scratchy character and a very abundant mineral
- This soothsayer is used to make crystal balls
- Amethyst was once believed to stop people from getting drunk

I'm an abrasive character—don't rub me the wrong way. Because my grains form sand, people see me as a beach bum with a sunny disposition. The secret of my success is my durability. You just can't get rid of me. I'm a big part of so many rocks—especially granite—and even when my sandy grains are worn down, they eventually get incorporated into new rocks, such as sandstone. When rocks are metamorphosed, I often migrate into milky white bands of pure quartz.

Although I'm no longer used to make sandpaper, I am the major source for making glass. And I'm used to measure time with my amazing powers of piezoelectricity. When under pressure, I vibrate with an electric rhythm, which is used to keep time in electronic clocks.

- Made of: silicon dioxide
- Chemical formula: $SiO_2$
- Hardness: 7
- Color: variable
- Crystal system: trigonal
- Look-alike: adularia (form of Feldspar)

Quartz

# Opal

## Mineral Gang

- This mischievous and colorful fellow has no internal structure
- Not a true mineral, Opal is a hardened silica gel
- This noncrystalline is South Australia's official gemstone

I play a game with light, which makes me shimmer like a pearl. I'm made up of tiny, see-through spheres that break up the light hitting me, making it bend and causing me to glisten. I am not a mineral but a silica gel. Hot, silica-rich water filters underground into gaps in the rock, where it hardens. That is why I'm found in fossils, in the spaces left by dead animals.

- Made of: hydrated silica
- Chemical formula: $SiO_2 \cdot nH_2O$
- Hardness: 5.5–6
- Color: milky white
- Crystal system: trigonal
- Look-alike: Agate

# Agate

## Mineral Gang

- A captivating banded mineral first found in Greece
- Ancient Greeks thought agate could calm troubled minds
- Made of quartz—Earth's third-most-abundant mineral

I'm a refined fellow with a history. I once had many uses, from curing scorpion stings to increasing powers of speech. These days, I am used to polish leather and crush chemicals in laboratories. I'm a fine-grained, milky, and hard microcrystalline form of quartz. I form my banded varieties inside air pockets in solid lava, when water deposits layers of silica, each in a different color.

- Made of: silica
- Chemical formula: $SiO_2$
- Hardness: 7
- Color: variable
- Crystal system: trigonal, hexagonal
- Look-alike: Opal

# Feldspar

## Mineral Gang

- This family makes up more than 60 percent of Earth's crust
- Rock made only of plagioclase feldspar is called anorthosite
- The mountains on the Moon are made of anorthosite

We form two mineral families: the K-feldspars and the plagioclase feldspars. Between us, we are the world's most abundant minerals and make up almost two-thirds of Earth's crust. We have been found in meteorites and across the solar system. We crystallize out of liquid magma and form a major part of most metamorphic, igneous, and sedimentary rocks. We are found in ornamental buildings and many household cleaners.

K-feldspars contain potassium and are known as alkali feldspars. They grace Granite with the pink sheen it takes in sunlight. The plagioclases are found in the more acid igneous rocks that are thrown out of Earth's continents. Unusually pale, there are copious amounts of them on the Moon.

- Made of: aluminum silicate
- Chemical formula: $KAlSi_3O_8$
- Hardness: 6–6.5
- Color: white, pink, yellow
- Crystal system: monoclinic, triclinic
- Look-alikes: Quartz, scapolite

Feldspar

# Olivine

## Mineral Gang

- This high-pressure honey is a major component of peridotite
- Takes its name from its unearthly olive green color
- Its gemstone, peridot, was a favorite with the ancient Egyptians

Looking like a green crystal of kryptonite, I'm totally far out. Though one of Earth's most common minerals, I can also be found on the Moon, Mars, in meteorites, and on the comet Wild 2. I don't make shapely crystals, but the atoms in my crystal lattice are closely packed, so I resist pressure. I can survive at pressures equivalent to 250 mi. (400km) deep within Earth. I am the most abundant mineral in Earth's mantle, where I am semiliquid. Huge bodies of me, bubbling like hot chocolate, drive Earth's tectonic plates around.

Two pints (1L) of my crushed crystals can absorb the carbon dioxide released by burning 2 pt. (1L) of oil. The reaction forms heat, so I could create power AND remove carbon dioxide from the atmosphere—the ultimate green dream!

- Made of: magnesium iron silicate
- Chemical formula: $(Mg, Fe)_2SiO_4$
- Hardness: 6.5–7
- Color: olive green
- Crystal system: orthorhombic
- Look-alike: diopside

Olivine

# Tourmaline

## Mineral Gang

- A glassy beauty who comes in a bamboozling variety of colors
- Lollipop crystals of green and pink are called "watermelon"
- The most common tourmaline is schorl

We're big, brash, bold, and beautiful . . . and we contain boron. A truly global phenomenon, our name is from the Sinhalese (Sri Lankan) word for "gem pebbles," and the Russian czars prized us.

Chemically, we're one complex mineral. There is space in our crystal makeup for a vast selection of metals, and we bring different talents to the mix. Our most common variety is black, but we can also be pink, red, or blue. We can have several colors on a single crystal or be green on the outside and pink in the middle. We can change color when seen from different angles. The tricks we play with light make us a good material for optical polarizing filters. We have piezoelectric properties, like Quartz, which makes us useful in depth-sounding devices on ships.

- Made of: crystal silicates
- Chemical formúla: very complex
- Hardness: 7–7.5
- Color: variable
- Crystal system: trigonal
- Look-alike: Apatite

Tourmaline

# Augite

## Mineral Gang

- This fire-loving mineral dresses in combat colors
- Happy to go with the flow, it changes its composition easily
- Earth's mantle rocks are made mostly of olivine and pyroxene

I am the most common member of the pyroxene (say "pie-rox-seen") gang. I'm a chunky, dull-looking, greenish-black character found in dark fine-grained igneous rocks such as basalt, diorite, and Moon rocks. I can alter my composition easily by adding different metals to my crystal lattice, but no matter what, I always carry my trademark crystal structure.

- Made of: silicate
- Chemical formula: $(Ca, Mg, Fe)SiO_3$
- Hardness: 5–6
- Color: black, dark green
- Crystal system: monoclinic
- Look-alike: Hornblende

# Hornblende

## Mineral Gang

- This dark and dusky mineral has one of the coolest names
- Hornblende is just one of many amphibole minerals
- Called garbage cans because they have so many compositions

My German name refers to my dazzling, devilish looks. I'm a member of the amphiboles, a group of dark silicon-based minerals. It's easy to get us mixed up with the pyroxenes, but our crystal faces meet at angles greater than 90 degrees. I occur in crystal blades within many different metamorphic and igneous rocks, including granite and basalt.

- Made of: silicate
- Chemical formula: very complex
- Hardness: 5–6
- Color: black, white tints
- Crystal system: monoclinic
- Look-alike: Augite

# Mica

## Mineral Gang

- Smooth dude who comes apart at the seams when it's hot
- Flakes of mica in rocks shimmer like scales on a fish's body
- *Mica* comes from the Latin words for "shine" and "glitter"

Even under a microscope, my crystal structure is so flat and laid-back that it has no bumps. This makes me good at cleaving (breaking apart along my crystal planes). Some might call me a flake, but I take pride in my ability to split, and geologists say my cleavage is "perfect."

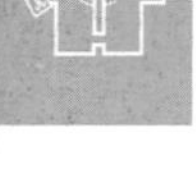

I am found in all rocks—my flakes sparkle in schist. My most common form is called muscovite, from *Muscovy*, the old word for Russia. Windows were once made of me, and I am still used for some windows on boilers and Geiger counters because I am very resistant to heat. I am also resistant to electric currents, which makes me useful in high-voltage electronic components such as capacitors. These two talents combined make me a great protective sheath for electric circuits because I won't melt in a fire.

- Made of: silicate
- Chemical formula: very complex
- Hardness: 2.5–3
- Color: brown
- Crystal system: monoclinic
- Look-alike: vermiculite

Mica

# Serpentine

## Mineral Gang

- Most commonly found in highly altered metamorphic zones
- A zombie who invades minerals and changes their structures
- Famous serpentines can be seen at Lizard Point in Cornwall, U.K.

People say there's something reptilian about me. Maybe it's my mottled surface that reminds people of snakeskin, or the greasy sheen I can take when my surfaces are freshly exposed. My crystal structure of flat silica sheets allows for a wide range of compositions, mostly of delicate greenish hues. Some of my many varieties, such as lizardite, can be carved into ornaments and polished to look almost as gorgeous as Jade.

Geologists call me a secondary mineral because I'm formed from another mineral. When ground water travels through rocks, I slip inside other minerals and take over. It's easy for atoms to slip into my crystal structure, so the chemical changes occur quickly and the original mineral morphs to my design. My favorite victim is Olivine.

- Made of: silicate hydroxide
- 
  Formula: $(Mg, Fe, Ni)_3Si_2O_5(OH)_4$
- Hardness: 2.5–5.5
- Color: olive green, yellow, red, black
- Crystal system: monoclinic
- Look-alikes: Peridotite, Talc

Serpentine

# Talc

## Mineral Gang

- A very useful mineral whose weakness is its strength
- Often found mixed with serpentine and calcite
- Made into a soothing powder to sprinkle on babies' bottoms

I'm a big softy. I am at the bottom of the pile when it comes to hardness, but I have tons of uses. I'm found in lubricants, paints, ceramics, plastics, and rubber, but I'm best known in talcum powder. I hang out in low-grade metamorphic rocks such as schist. I can be cut into without cracking, making me ideal for carving, which is why I'm used in soapstone ornaments.

- Made of: hydrous magnesium silicate
- Chemical formula: $Mg_3Si_4O_{10}(OH)_2$
- Hardness: 1
- Color: white
- Crystal system: monoclinic
- Look-alike: Serpentine

# Kaolinite

## Mineral Gang

- A down-to-earth mineral made of microscopic crystals
- A reaction of mica and/or feldspar to water can form it
- Can contain uranium, making it mildly radioactive

I am the workhorse of the mineral world. It may be unglamorous to be a clay mineral, but I'm proud of my usefulness. My tiny crystals are used in a paste to make china, clay, and toothpaste and are found in light bulbs, paints, and cosmetics. I provide the gloss in shiny magazine paper and soothe upset stomachs. I'm even used to add bulk to candy bars!

- Made of: hydrous aluminum silicate
- Chemical formula: $Al_2Si_2O_5 \cdot (OH)_4$
- Hardness: 2–2.5
- Color: white
- Crystal system: triclinic
- Look-alikes: clay minerals

# Garnet

## Mineral Gang

- This total stud is a semiprecious stone found all over the world
- There are a total of 15 different types of garnets
- The rarest garnet is the blue garnet of Bekily, Madagascar

I am a metamorphic marvel that you can find in many colors. My most well-known and recognizable color is pomegranate red. Hard and lumpy, I stick out of rock like a jeweled wart, and with my well-defined faces and edges, I could be described as a poor man's ruby.

There's no breaking me: I'm so hard that I'll stand my ground until I shatter instead of splitting, and I refuse to change chemically, too. I form during periods of upheaval in Earth, when mountains are being formed and the crust is being crushed and heated up. My bright red varieties are like the glowing embers of Earth's fires in rocks—and because I won't change, I act as a built-in temperature gauge that tells geologists the heat at which rocks were baked.

- Made of: silicate
- Chemical formula: complex silicate
- Hardness: 6.5–7.5
- Color: deep red, blue
- Crystal system: cubic
- Look-alike: spinel

Garnet

# Gypsum

## Mineral Gang

- This spooky mineral is the leftover residue when oceans dry up
- Also known as satin spar, desert rose, and plaster of Paris
- It patches over all sorts of defects in walls when redecorating

Soft, silky, and smooth, I am the desert rose. I am the deposits of hot springs and sea brine when the oceans evaporate. My powdery sands are bleached, super dry and ghostly white. White Sands in New Mexico is a huge expanse of dunes made of me. These gentle gypsum sands were the test site of the world's first atom bomb. Not much farther south in Mexico I have created the world's largest crystals in the Cave of Crystals.

Humans have found many uses for my milky softness, from mortar for cement, blackboard chalk, and fertilizer to plaster for the walls inside houses. While I am still wet, I can be molded into all sorts of shapes that then set hard. I also make your house safer because I'm extremely fire resistant. I'm the DIY king! Beat that!

- Made of: hydrated calcium sulfate
- Chemical formula: $CaSO_4{\cdot}2H_2O$
- Hardness: 1.5–2
- Color: colorless, white
- Crystal system: monoclinic
- Look-alikes: celestite, epsomite

Gypsum

# Calcite

## Mineral Gang

- A lovely transparent mineral that comes in many forms
- This party animal throws shapes such as the "dogtooth"
- It's often thought to crust up your faucets, but that's aragonite

There are two sides to my character: I'm completely essential for life on Earth yet totally self-effacing. I am all around you, but I go mostly unnoticed. I'm a beautiful mineral but as cold and distant as an ice queen.

There are tons of me dissolved in the world's water. Many oceangoing creatures extract me from the water to build their protective shells. Plankton, red algae, starfish, reef-building animals, clams, snails, and other shelled beasts would all be naked without me. I also find my way into sedimentary limestone, chalk rocks, and metamorphic marble. I am the one that makes your water hard. I make up for this with some flashy crystals. My top crystal, Iceland spar, shows double refraction, where anything seen through it appears twice.

- Made of: calcium carbonate
- Chemical formula: $CaCO_3$
- Hardness: 3
- Color: colorless, white
- Crystal system: hexagonal
- Look-alike: dolomite

Calcite

# Malachite

## Mineral Gang

- This gorgeous mineral has a long and illustrious history
- A source mineral for the valuable metal copper
- Spearheaded the search for rocks with metal-bearing minerals

I am the green goddess. You can get lost in my gleaming green depths and dark swirls. When polished, I am just too pretty to be destroyed. Nevertheless, I was the first ore to be smelted to produce copper. I was also used as a medicinal eye paint in ancient Egypt and as a base for green paints. These days, I am still used to color stained glass.

- Made of: copper carbonate
- Chemical formula: $Cu_2CO_3(OH)_2$
- Hardness: 3.5–4
- Color: bright green with bands
- Crystal system: monoclinic
- Look-alike: chrysocolla

# Apatite

## Mineral Gang

- One of the few minerals used by biological organisms
- Apatite fertilizers starve plants of nitrogen and alter their taste
- Mineral collectors have a great "apatite" for violet apatite!

I'm like a social club: everyone is welcome. My family members can be green, blue, violet, purple, white, yellow, rose, or clear—but they all have the same structure. With a little gemming up on me, you'll learn that I am a major part of your tooth enamel and bones. I am also the world's main source of phosphate, used in fertilizers, and I can stop fungi from destroying crops.

- Made of: phosphate
- Chemical formula: $Ca_5(PO_4)_3F$
- Hardness: 5

- Color: pale blue, green, yellow
- Crystal system: hexagonal
- Look-alike: Corundum

# Fluorite

## Mineral Gang

- A salty dog with lovely crystals, but too soft to be a gemstone
- Fluorite was once thought to give wine its lip-smacking flavor
- The best-known "Blue John" mines are in Castleton, England

I'm a colorful character with plenty of tales to tell. I come in purples, violets, greens, yellows, pinks, and a handsome banded variety called "Blue John." I even fluoresce under UV lights. I would like to join the Little Gems, but I'm too soft and easily defaced.

I was first noticed when people began to smelt iron ore (after 2000 B.C.). I melt easily, and when added to molten iron ore, I bind to the useless parts so that they can be removed. First-century Romans made pitchers and cups from me. Since then, I have been added to water to prevent kidney disease, have become a major component of nonstick coatings, and am used to make high-octane fuels. Lenses made from me are more transparent than glass and eliminate color distortion.

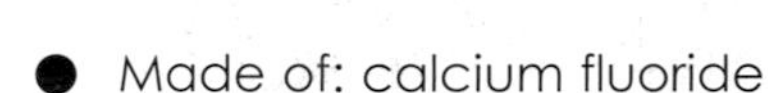

- Made of: calcium fluoride
- Chemical formula: $CaF_2$
- Hardness: 4
- Color: variable
- Crystal system: cubic
- Look-alike: halite

Fluorite

# CHAPTER 6

## The Purists

Also known as Native Elements, the Purists are a small band of puritans. Unlike most minerals, they are made up of only one type of atom and are unearthed in the purest form possible—one element. No substance can be simpler; it's elementary! These are the chemicals that make up the periodic table, including metals and nonmetals. They make the world's finest ores. These perfectionists also include Earth's greatest treasures. Some members of the Little Gems gang, such as Diamond, are honorary members of the Purists.

Sulfur

Graphite

Silver

Gold

Arsenic

# Sulfur

## The Purists

- A sickly element from volcanic zones that can cause acid rain
- 85 percent of the sulfur mined is used to make sulfuric acid
- Jupiter's moon Io has volcanoes that erupt sulfur gas

Fire and brimstone! I spew out of foul jets from volcanoes and hot springs, and I'm a real little stinker. My pure form is odorless, but when I combine with hydrogen in hydrogen sulfide, I reek of rotten eggs. I make your nose water because on contact with your damp nasal passages, I form stinging sulfuric acid.

I'm found in galena, pyrite, and many meteorites, but on my own you can't miss me—I like bright lemon yellows. Picking up chunks of me from a volcano crater in clouds of lethal gas is the most dangerous way of mining me. These days, I'm mostly mined by pumping hot water underground. I'm used in gunpowder, matches, pesticides, and fungicides, but mostly I'm used to make sulfuric acid—the most useful product in the chemical industry.

- Made of: sulfur
- Symbol: S
- Hardness: 1.5–2.5
- Color: bright yellow
- Crystal system: orthorhombic
- Look-alike: autunite

Sulfur

# Graphite

## The Purists

- A cool customer who conducts electricity well without melting
- Human-made graphene is the world's strongest material
- Famously pure deposits were mined in Borrowdale, England

I'm the dirty brother of Diamond—the black sheep of the carbon family. I have the same composition as Diamond, but my carbon atoms aren't packed so tightly. Where Diamond is hard, I am soft and slimy, and where he is gleaming bright, I am greasy black. I am found mostly as layers in metamorphic marble rock, formed when fossils and organic matter in limestone are lightly toasted.

My slippery softness means that I leave a mark on almost any surface, which is why I'm used to make pencils. This same buttery quality makes me a fantastic machine oil—I'm a true handyman. I am also used as control rods in nuclear reactors to mop up excess neutrons, and I govern the ferocity of nuclear-fission reactions. I'm used in arc lamps, batteries, motors, and generators, too.

- Made of: carbon
- Symbol: C
- Hardness: 1–2
- Color: black, silvery gray
- Crystal system: hexagonal
- Look-alike: manganite

Graphite

# Silver

## The Purists

- A Purist often found alloyed with gold, sulfur, or arsenic
- This sparky guy is the world's greatest conductor of electricity
- Often has the code E174 when used as a food additive

White and shining, I am one of the oldest precious metals. Sadly, I tarnish in air, leaving black stains of silver sulfide. My pure form is rare. I am minted as coins and used for jewelry, cutlery, and ornaments. I am a catalyst (I help create chemical reactions) in many industrial processes. Bacteria and fungi can't stand me, so I've been used to treat wounds.

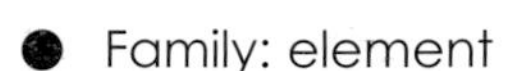

- Family: element
- Symbol: Ag
- Hardness: 2.5–3
- Color: silvery white
- Crystal system: cubic
- Look-alikes: Silver sulfides

# Gold

## The Purists

- A heavyweight found in pure nuggets, usually in quartz veins
- An ultra softy who can be beaten into leafy sheets
- The U.S. Federal Reserve holds 3 percent of all gold ever mined

I am pure class—and I remain unblemished by the passage of time. I am a buttery softy, so I need to be alloyed to other metals to make me hard enough for use in dentistry and electronics. A coating of me just one atom thick helps protect satellites and astronauts' space suits from heat in space. When it comes to conduction, I am almost as good as Silver, but I don't tarnish!

- Family: element
- Symbol: Au
- Hardness: 2.5–3
- Color: bright golden yellow
- Crystal system: cubic
- Look-alike: Pyrite

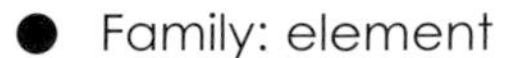

# Arsenic

## The Purists

- A toxic traitor who gets mixed up in spiteful goings-on
- Smells like garlic when heated or hit with a hammer
- Also used as a pesticide on fruit crops, so wash those apples!

With my pleasingly rounded bumps, I look like an inviting bunch of grapes, but I'm a crushing letdown. My gray metallic berries will leave a bitter taste in your mouth and cause your body to shut down completely. I'm a notorious criminal with a long rap sheet. I'm often called the "poison of kings" because for a long time I was the toxin of choice for the ruling classes when they wanted to bump one another off. These days, tests can detect arsenic poisoning, so I'm rarely used for murder.

I have also been hard on artists. I was used to make "emerald green," a favorite color of artists Claude Monet (who went blind) and Vincent van Gogh (who went crazy). Today, I'm more likely to be found as a semiconductor in electronic transistors.

- Family: element
- Symbol: As
- Hardness: 3.5
- Color: dark gray
- Crystal system: rhombohedral
- Look-alike: Silver

Arsenic

# CHAPTER 7
## Little Gems

This crew dazzles and sparkles. They are an exclusive club with only 130 members—even though they're little more than normal minerals, these guys form exceptionally fine-looking crystals. These rare beauties are valuable—millions of poor people mine them so that only a handful of the very rich can wear them. When cut and polished, the Little Gems become gemstones. Gemstones are judged on the "four Cs"—color, cut, clarity, and carat (weight). Size does matter with Little Gems—the bigger they are, the more valuable!

Diamond

Emerald (Beryl)

Corundum

Topaz

Jade

# Diamond

## Little Gems

- A rare beauty, mined from volcanic feeder pipes
- A slow developer, this gem is never less than one billion years old
- Pressures are so great on Neptune that it rains diamonds!

Showing off my dazzling winsome faces, I drive the ladies wild. As the hardest mineral on Earth, I am completely resistant to chemical attacks and never get dulled by scratches and nicks. Diamonds really are forever! I form in volcanic pipes of kimberlite, but I can be dredged up out of riverbeds and off the ocean floor. I'm so treasured that wars are fought to control the fields where I'm found.

I'm 100 percent pure carbon, but unlike Graphite, I form insanely good-looking crystals. The conditions in which I form are found in only two situations on Earth: 87–118 mi. (140–190km) below the surface of stable continents and at meteor impact sites. I am hard and can slice through tough stuff such as solid rock. Only a diamond can cut another diamond, so I'm used to cut other gemstones.

- Family: element
- Symbol: C
- Hardness: 10
- Color: colorless, white, pink, yellow
- Crystal system: cubic
- Look-alikes: zircon, synthetic gems

Diamond

# Emerald (Beryl)

## Little Gems

- Fine examples of emeralds are super rare and seriously valuable
- The largest crystal ever found was in Madagascar, at 1,182 lbs.
- Aquamarine is another gemstone-quality variety of beryl

Vivid and glowing with internal fires, I'm a classy and expensive kind of lady. You can get lost in my gorgeous green depths. My original Semitic name is the bewitching sounding "Izmargad," but you can call me Beryl!

My deep green comes from traces of chromium in my crystal structure, but despite my outward beauty, I have many defects. Other minerals creep inside my crystals in inclusions, and I am riven with fissures and surface cracks. Sometimes inclusions make me even more valuable, such as organic material trapped in star-shaped trapiche emeralds. Strange beliefs surround me like flocks of ravens. People once claimed I drove off evil spirits, prevented epileptic seizures, and even, when popped into the mouth, stopped chronic diarrhea!

- Family: beryl
- Chemical formula: $Be_3Al_2Si_6O_{18}$
- Hardness: 7.5–8
- Color: green
- Crystal system: hexagonal
- Look-alike: Tourmaline

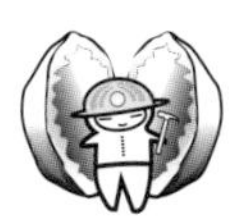

Emerald (Beryl)

# Corundum

## Little Gems

- This Little Gem makes both lovely rubies and sultry sapphires
- A difficult fellow whose best examples come from conflict zones
- "Pigeon blood" rubies are the most highly prized rubies of all

I'm truly classy—I'm the jewel of choice for kings and emperors. You probably know me better as my two varieties, ruby and sapphire. It can be difficult to distinguish rubies from other minerals. In the 1800s, the "Black Prince's Ruby" on the Queen of England's crown—which has been around since 1367—was discovered to be a spinel mineral (magnesium aluminum oxide) instead!

I'm a tough cookie—second only to Diamond. I don't wear easily, so riverbeds and beaches are good places to find me. I easily scratch most other minerals, so I'm used as a sandpaper abrasive and to machine metals. Sapphires and rubies often come from regions such as India, Sri Lanka, and Myanmar (Burma). At 335 lbs. (152kg), the largest corundum crystal came from the Transvaal, South Africa.

- Family: hematite
- Chemical formula: $Al_2O_3$
- Hardness: 9
- Color: gray, green, red, blue, yellow
- Crystal system: hexagonal
- Look-alikes: Emerald, Apatite

Corundum

# Topaz

## Little Gems

- A hard mineral occurring in acid igneous rocks such as granite
- Colorful varieties mined in the Urals are used as gemstones
- A whopping 5,902-lb. crystal was found in Mozambique

Crystal clear and sparkly bright, I am a Brazilian beauty often mistaken for Diamond. Like a carnival queen, I come in a dazzling array of colors. My pink variety is loved so much that people often heat up cheaper yellow crystals to make them turn pink. Although I'm a hard nut, I can split, so you have to handle me with care when cutting me.

- Family: topaz
- Chemical formula: $Al_2SiO_4(F,OH)_2$
- Hardness: 8
- Color: clear, blue, yellow, pink
- Crystal system: orthorhombic
- Look-alike: zircon

# Jade

## Little Gems

- A gorgeous green gem, found in metamorphic schist
- Was the symbol of status and power in ancient China
- Major deposits of me can be found in China and New Zealand

I'm a milky green mineral, often found with Talc and Serpentine in metamorphic rocks. (Two similar minerals—jadeite and nephrite—are both called jade.) My toughness makes me ideal for carving, and I was revered in Asian society, where I was thought to hold cosmic energy. Many intricate ornaments were carved from me. These days, such ornaments are priceless. Like me!

- Family: pyroxene
- Chemical formula: very complex
- Hardness: 6.5–7
- Color: cream to dark green
- Crystal system: monoclinic
- Look-alike: amphibole

# CHAPTER 8

## Fossils

While not rocks or minerals, these oldies but goodies are an important part of the story of life. They are the remains of plants and animals that once roamed the earth and swam in the seas. As old as the rocks themselves, they form layers in the bedrock that can be studied and that give us clues to the past. Eighteenth-century scientists realized that fossils were the remains of organisms that had once lived, and their presence in deeply buried layers of strata showed that life on Earth has an ancient history—stretching back more than 3.5 billion years.

Replacement Fossil

Trace Fossil

Impression Fossil

Amber

# Replacement Fossil

## Fossils

- This old rocker is once-living matter that has turned to stone
- A sure-fire way for extinct organisms to leave their mark on Earth
- Body cells are sometimes preserved, showing how life worked

I'm your classic fossil, and a handsome treasure, too. I offer the only way for animals and plants to live on millions of years after they die—by turning them to stone. My secret spell is mineral-rich waters creeping through the rocks.

As organic parts of a once-alive thing rot, minerals move in and take their place. This is called permineralization. Minerals can replace every tiny bit, as in petrified wood. Some of my most impressive varieties occur when the waters dissolve the original shells or bones, leaving a cast that is filled by minerals. The best examples are ammonites—the oceangoing creatures that look like curlicue ram's horns and went extinct along with the dinosaurs 65 million years ago.

Replacement Fossil

# Trace Fossil

■ Fossils

- This old fossil captures the activities of ancient animals
- The main chance of squishy animals like worms being preserved
- Most "traces," or footprints, come from sea creatures

Follow in my footsteps and I'll show you the secret lives of extinct animals. I am the record of the day-to-day business of beasties many millions of years ago—their tracks and trails, the signs of their activities, and even their bowel movements!

To be left behind in the rocks, I have to be made by creatures moving and operating in soft mud that later hardens. The first examples of me are slither marks from simple worms living about 570 million years ago. As time passed, I became more complicated—worms began to burrow, trilobites scuttled, and, eventually, dinosaurs stomped. My dino tracks are my most famous fossils—they have shown herds of plant-eating dinosaurs protecting their young from stalking predators.

Trace Fossil

# Impression Fossil

Fossils

- A fair-minded fossil who redresses the balance for softy animals
- 2-D imprints of organisms, without organic matter
- You can see pores and skeletons of animals in these impressions

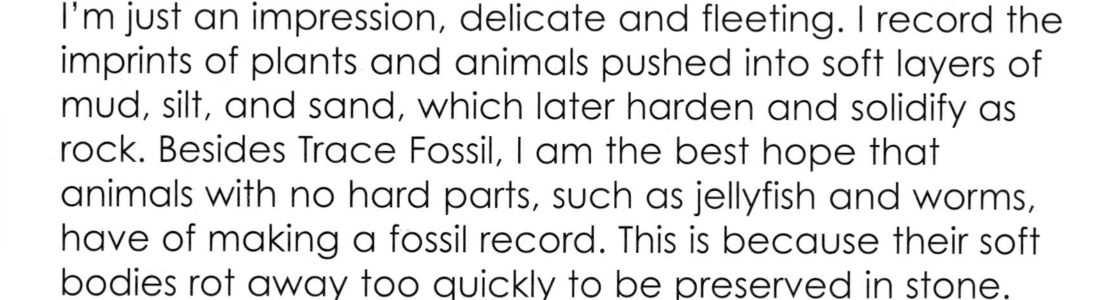

I'm just an impression, delicate and fleeting. I record the imprints of plants and animals pushed into soft layers of mud, silt, and sand, which later harden and solidify as rock. Besides Trace Fossil, I am the best hope that animals with no hard parts, such as jellyfish and worms, have of making a fossil record. This is because their soft bodies rot away too quickly to be preserved in stone.

My best examples are flat things, such as leaves and fern fronds. In rare finds I show the intricate internal structures of plants. My impressions have also given scientists clues about how some ancient animals looked, including fantastic discoveries showing the warty skin of dinosaurs.

Impression Fossil

# Amber

## Fossils

- A real golden glory—this character is fossilized tree resin
- Neither mineral nor fossil, it's often treated as a gemstone
- A fossil collector, it's the ultimate preserver of tiny life

With my warm honey tones, I look like I have sunlight locked inside me, preserved forever. I get my golden glow from hardened resin from trees, but I'm no sap! Tree resin is semisolid sticky stuff, squirted out by a plant's protective layer of cells.

I could not exist until pine trees evolved, so I'm a young gun. Yet in my short life I've been busy. Slow-flowing and sticky, I've snared twigs, leaves, bits of wood, pieces of wings, whole insects such as flies and ants, and even small vertebrates such as frogs! There was an idea that you could extract DNA from my preserved beasties, but that was just a pipe dream. However, I'm also a sparky guy. Old-school scientists got a charge by rubbing rods made of me to build up static electricity.

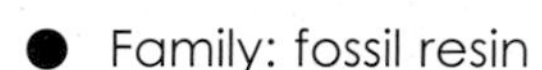

- Family: fossil resin
- Symbol: $C_{10}H_{16}O$
- Hardness: 2–2.5

- Color: orange-yellow, brown
- Crystal system: amorphous
- Look-alikes: copal, plastic

Amber

# INDEX

# GLOSSARY

**Aquifer** A porous rock formation that holds large amounts of water in an underground well.

**Bedding plane** A horizontal layer of sedimentary rock, compressed under deposits formed above it.

**Chemical sediment** Matter formed as minerals crystallize, where the water is rich in particles.

**Clastic** Describes rocks made from fragments of older rocks.

**Crystal system** A classification method for identifying crystals, dividing them into seven groups: isometric, tetragonal, hexagonal, trigonal, orthorhombic, monoclinic, and triclinic.

**Erosion** The process by which a rock is worn away.

**Extrusive** A term to describe igneous rock that has poured out onto Earth's surface and solidified.

**Foliation** Leaflike layers of rock that have strong mineral bands running through them.

**Fluoresce** To emit light or another type of radiation.

**Friable** Describes a substance that crumbles easily.

**Gemstone** A precious or semiprecious stone, especially when cut and polished.

**Hardness** The resistance of the surface of an object to scratching and abrasion. This is measured on the Mohs scale of hardness.

**Igneous** A type of rock formed from molten rock (magma) as it cools and solidifies.

**Mantle convection** The slow, creeping movement of Earth's rocky mantle as a result of gravitational forces.

**Metamorphic** A type of rock formed from the transforming of old rock by varying amounts of heat and pressure.

**Midocean ridge** An underwater mountain range where tectonic plates meet and form a valley (rift).

**Mineral** A naturally occurring substance that is solid, inorganic, and crystalline in form.

**Mohs scale** *see* **Hardness**.

# GLOSSARY

**Nodule** A small rounded lump.

**Piezoelectricity** A process where some crystalline substances (for example, quartz) generate an electrical charge when compressed.

**Plate tectonics** A theory explaining the movement of Earth's plates.

**Pores** Small holes in rocks.

**Sediment** Matter rich in minerals that have been deposited over time by rivers and glaciers.

**Sedimentary** A type of rock formed by weathering or chemical buildup as mineral particles are deposited, buried, and squashed into layers.

**Semiconductor** A solid material that has some electrical conductivity.

**Sorted** Describes the uniformity of grain sizes within a sedimentary rock.

**Subduction zone** An area at a tectonic plate boundary where one tectonic plate is sinking beneath another.

**Tectonic** Relating to the movements in Earth's crust.